Sylvia Stark

A PIONEER

Sylvia Stark

Stark

A PIONEER

A Biography by
VICTORIA SCOTT & ERNEST JONES

Illustrated by
KAREN LEWIS

OPEN HAND PUBLISHING INC.

Seattle, Washington

OPEN HAND PUBLISHING INC.
P.O. Box 22048, Seattle, WA 98122
206-323-2187 • FAX 206-323-2188

Distributed by **The Subterranean Company**
P.O. Box 160, 265 S. Fifth St., Monroe, Oregon 97456
503-847-5274 • TOLL-FREE ORDERS 800-274-7826 • FAX 503-847-6018

Book and cover design:
Deb Figen • ART & DESIGN SERVICES • Seattle, Washington

Library of Congress Cataloging-in-Publication Data

Scott, Victoria, 1958-
Sylvia Stark, a pioneer : a biography / by Victoria Scott & Ernest Jones ; illustrated by Karen Lewis. -- 1st ed.
p. cm.
Includes bibliographical references.
Summary : Chronicles the life of a woman who was born a slave in Missouri in 1839, moved with her family to California, and later lived on a small island off the coast of British Columbia until she was 105.
ISBN 0-940880-37-7 (cloth cover) : $12.95 -- ISBN 0-940880-38-5 (pbk.) : $6.95
1. Stark, Sylvia, b. 1839--Juvenile literature. 2. Pioneers--British Columbia--Saltspring Island--Biography--Juvenile literature. 3. Saltspring Island (B. C.)--Biography--Juvenile literature. 4. Frontier and pioneer life--British Columbia--Saltspring Island--Juvenile literature 5. Pioneers, Black--British Columbia--Saltspring Island--Biography--Juvenile literature. 6. Pioneers--California--Biography--Juvenile literature. 7. Afro-American Pioneers--California--Biography--Juvenile literature. 8. Frontier and pioneer life--California--Juvenile literature. 9. California--Gold discoveries--Juvenile literature. [1. Stark, Sylvia, b. 1839. 2. Afro-Americans--Biography. 3. Frontier and pioneer life.] I. Jones, Ernest, 1958- . II. Lewis, Karen, ill. III. Title.
F1089.S2S727 1992
971. 1' 28--dc20
[B]   91-46236
                                                                     CIP
                                                                      AC

FIRST EDITION

Printed in the United States of America
96 95 94   8 7 6 5 4 3 2

Acknowledgments

A couple of months after Victoria and I decided to put this book together, it dawned on us that getting a book published is a much more complicated process than we had anticipated. We received help and motivation from many people in order to get it done.

We are grateful to Sylvia Stark's descendents, Ethel and Yvonne Claibourne and Myrtle Holloman, for their helpful conversations with us and for permission to use family photographs. Sylvia Stark's daughter Marie wrote down many stories as she heard them from her mother. Mrs. Holloman, Marie's daughter, gave us permission to use these stories, and they are the basis for this book. Our research was greatly helped by Brian Young, Reference Services Supervisor at the British Columbia Archives and Record Service. Thanks to Brenda Brock and Deborah Scott for their reading and rereading of our manuscript; and to Rebecca Allen, Literacy Coordinator for the Seattle Public Library; and Bobby Hollingsworth and the people at Seattle Goodwill Adult Learning Center who helped us learn about writing for New Readers. We are also grateful to our publisher, P. Anna Johnson and the book designer, Deb Figen.

Karen Lewis spent an incredible amount of time researching the subject matter before she produced these illustrations. Her work has transformed this book.

This book was funded, in part, by a grant from the Washington Commission for the Humanities.

These are some of the people who helped us along the way. We are grateful to everyone who has given us support.

**This book is dedicated to our families,
especially the newest member,
Sarah Scott Jamison.**

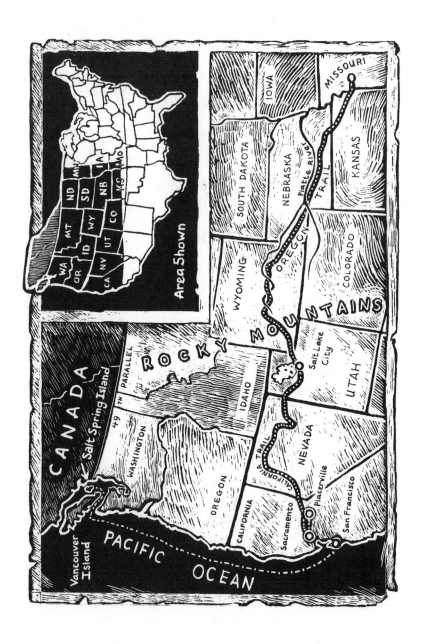

Table of Contents

Introduction

Tall trees and thick bushes cast shadows across the dark brown earth in Sylvia Stark's garden on Salt Spring Island. The spring air was cool. Daylight was fading. Sylvia's small garden plot was almost ready to be planted. Only a corner was left covered with fallen winter leaves and weeds.

Sylvia Stark stood in the weeds leaning on her hoe. She was a small woman, barely five feet tall. Her round face was wrinkled and her knuckles were swollen with age, but her eyes were bright. After resting for a moment, she began digging again. She was determined to finish preparing the garden for planting before sundown.

Sylvia moved slowly. Her back ached and she could not see very well. As she worked, she thought of all the gardens she had planted in her long life. Sylvia figured she had been planting gardens for ninety-five years, beginning with her mother's little patch back in Missouri.

Sylvia was born in Missouri in 1839. This was before the American Civil War, when slavery was legal. As a very young child, Sylvia lived with her mother and her brother and sister. Sylvia's mother had a little garden she called "my weeds." Sylvia remembered her mother bending over her greens in the hazy, washed-out heat of summer.

When Sylvia was twelve years old, she and her family moved to California in a covered wagon. Her mother made a beautiful garden in California. Wildflowers grew all around it. Sylvia carried water from the stream to water the plants.

Sylvia's first garden of her own was on Salt Spring Island, way up north in British Columbia, Canada. Sylvia was twenty-one years old when she moved to Salt Spring Island with her husband and two children. Cougar and bear lived in the thick forest that covered the island. There were only a few houses and no roads. Sylvia had only a small garden that year because she and her husband Louis had to clear the land by hand.

Sylvia lived on Salt Spring Island until she died at age 105. She and Louis farmed and raised six children on the island. Every year she grew enough food for her family for a whole winter.

This book is about Sylvia Stark's life. It is also about the history of North America and British Columbia. History is the story of people's lives and the changes in the world around them. Each of our lives is a story. The things we do and think are all a part of history.

• • • • •

Ernie and I had the idea to write a book about Sylvia Stark during a vacation in the Gulf Islands of British Columbia. We were kayaking and camping in the islands. We brought with us a book with information about each island.

Salt Spring Island, the largest of the Gulf Islands, was first settled in 1860 by about twenty families. At that time, only a few of the Gulf Islands had people living on them. Salt Spring Island was uninhabited, although the Cowichan and Salish Indians who lived on nearby islands sometimes visited it.

Nine of the twenty families that settled on Salt Spring were Black. Most of them were African-Americans who had left the United States and the American Territories in search of a place where they could live without fear and racism.

Ernie and I wondered about these people. Who were they? Where did they come from? And why did they move to the Canadian wilderness?

On our way home to Seattle, we stopped at the Provincial Museum Archive in Victoria, British Columbia. The archive is a library of old books and documents. We wanted to find out more about the Black pioneers on Salt Spring Island.

A man who worked there showed us "The Sylvia Stark Story," thirty pages of stories that Sylvia Stark told about growing up to her daughter Marie. After Sylvia died, Marie wrote down these stories about her mother's life.

A month later, Ernie and I went back to Salt Spring Island. The day we arrived, it rained four inches in twenty-four hours. The electricity went out on the island and the roads flooded. But it was worth the trip.

We went to a local restaurant called the Ship's Anchor. A few minutes later, two older Black women came in to eat lunch. Ernie and I looked at each other.

"It's your turn, Ernie." I whispered. "Ask them if they know anything about Sylvia Stark." Ernie is shy. I gave him a shove.

The women were very friendly. And we were in luck! They were Sylvia Stark's granddaughter, Mrs. Ethel Claibourne, and Mrs. Claibourne's daughter, Miss Yvonne Claibourne! Mrs. Claibourne invited us to their house the next day.

We spent the next afternoon talking with the Claibournes about their family's history. They told us about Sylvia Stark's bad-tempered husband, Louis, who was murdered in a dispute about mineral rights. They talked about Sylvia's son Willis, the cougar hunter, who lived his whole life on Salt Spring Island.

Mrs. Claibourne said Sylvia Stark was a tiny woman, but strong and determined. She earned money by selling eggs and milk, and she was very proud of her gardens. She often gave away extra vegetables.

Everybody on Salt Spring Island knew Sylvia Stark. They respected her. She and her husband taught their children something Sylvia learned from her parents: Do not accept being treated like slaves or second-class citizens. Know who you are and what you want, and don't take "No" for an answer!

On our drive back to Seattle we decided to make a book about Sylvia Stark's life. Neither of us had written a book before, but the story of Sylvia Stark was a very good place to start.

Willis Stark.
Photo courtesy of Myrtle Holloman.

Howard Estes.
Photo courtesy of Myrtle Holloman.

CHAPTER ONE

Early Childhood

Early Memories

Sylvia was born in Missouri in 1839, in a shed behind the big house where her mother worked. This shed was where her mother slept and read her Bible. The floor was dirt and light came in through the cracks in the walls, but Sylvia's mother and father welcomed their baby into the world and wrapped her in the tiny quilt Sylvia's mother had sewn by hand.

Sylvia's mother was named Hannah Estes. She lived in the household of a German baker named Charles Leopold. Sylvia's father, Howard Estes, lived outside of town. He was a cowboy on a ranch owned by a man named Tom Estes. Howard spent Sundays with his family. Both of Sylvia's parents were slaves. Sylvia had an older brother named Jackson. Two years after Sylvia was born, her sister Agnes was born in the same shed.

Howard and Hannah's African family names were lost when their parents were brought to the United States. Because they were slaves, they were called by the names of their masters. When Hannah married Howard, she changed her name from Leopold to Estes.

As soon as Sylvia, Jackson and Agnes were old enough to walk, they helped their mother. Sylvia's earliest memories were of working.

Sylvia helped her mother in the Leopolds' kitchen. Hannah stood Sylvia on a chair and tied the strings of a big apron around her neck. Sylvia dried the Leopolds' big plates carefully.

"Hold on tight, Sylvia," her mother said. "Don't drop that plate, or else!" Then Hannah pretended she was angry, like Mrs. Leopold, the master's wife. Sylvia laughed, but she was scared, too.

When Sylvia was older, she took care of the Leopold children. Sylvia could not go to school because there were no schools for African-American children. It was against the law to teach a Black person to read at that time. But when the Leopold children started learning to read, Sylvia listened and learned along with them. When they did their homework, she asked them questions. Sometimes she helped them figure out problems.

Sylvia Learns She Is a Slave

Sylvia learned that she was a slave one Christmas day when she was still very young. Sylvia, Jackson and Agnes were allowed to play with the Leopold children on Christmas day. All the children waited eagerly to go into the room with the Christmas tree. They crowded against the door, trying to peek through the keyhole. Sylvia was very small, and when the door opened, she snuck into the room first.

"Nigger, don't you know the white children always come first!" Mrs. Leopold screamed at Sylvia. Her arm shot out and she jerked Sylvia back by her collar. Sylvia choked with fear and surprise as she stared up at Mrs. Leopold's red face. Sylvia began to cry and her mother quickly carried her back to the kitchen.

"It's all right, baby," Hannah said to Sylvia. "You've got to act right around them. But don't believe it. You're no nigger. You are Sylvia, my baby girl."

After this, Sylvia stopped talking to most people except her family. She pretended that there were two Sylvias: a real one for her family and a pretend one to show white people. Sylvia felt safe only when she was with her mother and her family. Sylvia began to worry. "What will happen to me if Ma dies? Where will I go?"

Sylvia's mother and father were religious people. They took Sylvia, Jackson and Agnes to church every Sunday. They went to the same church as white people, but they had to sit in the back.

The minister preached to the Black people like a boss talking to his slaves. He said, "The Bible says: Servants, obey your masters." Hannah Estes knew this was not true religion. She taught her children that God did not make slavery. Hannah Estes refused to think of herself as a slave in church or at home.

One day Mrs. Leopold and Hannah Estes had a fight. Hannah was kneading bread when Mrs. Leopold told her to make a fire in the oven.

"I'm busy now. I will make the fire when I am through kneading dough," Hannah said.

"How dare you disobey my orders!" Mrs. Leopold screamed.

When Mr. Leopold came in, he got mad at Hannah. Mr. Leopold held a whip over Hannah, but he did not hit her. Mr. Leopold could see that Hannah would fight him with all her strength so he backed off. He liked Hannah and did not want to fight her, but he was afraid that people would hear he let his slaves talk back. He told both women not to fight.

Hannah heard Mr. Leopold telling other white people that he thought slavery was wrong. "I keep slaves because I have to. I can't run this bakery by myself," he said to customers. They crossed their arms and stared at him. Some white people hated Mr. Leopold because he spoke out publicly against slavery. This made Sylvia and her mother afraid. If Mr. Leopold died, then they would be sold to a slave trader.

Slave traders roamed all over the South. Sometimes they kidnapped Black people. Things were so bad that it was not safe for Black children to play outside their own homes. Sylvia ran away from white strangers. She knew that Black children were often kidnapped and sold to work in the cotton fields. Sometimes Sylvia did not even feel safe in her own bed.

Scarlet Fever

When Sylvia was ten, her sister Agnes became ill with scarlet fever. Two of the Leopold children also had the fever. The white children recovered from the fever, but Agnes died from it. Sylvia heard her mother arguing with the white doctor. He told her that Agnes died because Black children were weaker than white children.

"That's not true! My child was outside working in the cold rain even when she was burning up with fever!" Sylvia's mother said. Sylvia saw angry tears in her mother's eyes. "I didn't see you here checking her fever every day along with the white children's! The child wasn't even allowed to rest."

Sylvia's mother stood facing the doctor with her hands on her hips. The doctor's face grew red and his lips pressed into a thin line. Sylvia thought he would hit her mother. But Mr. Leopold stepped between them and hurried the doctor out.

Harriet

Soon after Agnes' death, a new slave, Harriet, joined the Leopold household. She was about fifteen years old. She was only five feet tall, but to young Sylvia she seemed big and strong. All her life, Sylvia remembered this young woman's spirit and determination. It was not long before Harriet and Mrs. Leopold began fighting. Every cruel word that Mrs. Leopold said to Harriet, Harriet tossed back. Soon everyone was whispering about Harriet's outspokenness. Some people thought she was brave, and others said she was foolish.

After a few months, Mrs. Leopold talked Mr. Leopold into selling Harriet to a slave breaker. Slave breakers were men who beat and tortured Black people until they stopped fighting back. But when the slave breaker tried to beat Harriet, she fought back. When he threatened to shoot her, she stood up to him and said, "Go ahead and shoot. I would rather die than be a slave to a man like you!"

He shot her in the foot. It healed slowly. Hannah Estes and Sylvia visited Harriet often until she got well. Harriet's spirit remained strong, and when her foot healed, she ran away. Later, they heard she had traveled the Underground Railroad to the North, to freedom. The Underground Railroad was a secret route that many people followed to escape slavery. Black and white people along the Railroad gave food and shelter to the runaways.

Sylvia told her daughter Marie this story years later. She said, "I like to think that our Harriet met Harriet Tubman, who led so many people to freedom along the Underground Railroad. They were so much alike."

CHAPTER TWO

Buying Freedom

The California Gold Rush

In 1848, a group of Miwok Indians working for two white men found gold in a river near San Francisco, California. They tried to keep it secret, but one year later everybody in North America had heard about gold in California. It was a gold rush!

People from all over North America traveled by wagon or boat to the California Territory to find gold and strike it rich. Between 1848 and 1852, 240,000 people moved to California. Some of them were African-Americans.

When the gold miners arrived in California, they needed food, clothes and homes. Miners paid for these things with gold. Mr. Tom Estes, Sylvia's father's boss, knew he could sell cattle for a lot of money in California. In 1849, Mr. Estes decided to send his two sons from Missouri to California with a herd of his cattle to sell.

Howard Estes Goes to California

Sylvia's father Howard Estes also heard about the gold rush. He knew slavery was illegal in the California Territory. Black people were mining alongside whites, and some of them were striking it rich. Howard Estes started making a plan for freedom for himself and his family. First he would get his master, Mr. Estes, to send him to California.

Late one afternoon, Howard and Mr. Estes rode up to the ranch after checking fences all day. Howard knew that Mr. Estes was angry at his son Ralph because the boy had lost three stray cattle that week.

"Boss, your sons are fine young cattlemen." Howard told Mr. Estes as they walked their horses to the barn. "I found those strays clear in the next county. Mister Ralph just didn't know how far a young steer will travel."

Mr. Estes did not say anything. He flung himself off his horse and sat down on a bale of hay. Howard tied the horses to a rail and began pulling off their saddles.

"Yes, sir. Takes time to learn to figure what a stray will do when it breaks loose. You have to know how they think. You've got to be two steps ahead of them."

Mr. Estes still said nothing, but Howard watched him chewing a piece of hay and thinking. Howard decided to let him chew a while longer.

Howard knew Mr. Estes' first thought was always about money. If Mr. Estes thought his sons would lose cattle on the way to California, he would send Howard with them. Howard Estes was a very skilled cowboy.

That night, Mr. Estes sat down with a piece of paper. He wrote down two numbers. One was possible losses from run-away cattle. The other was Howard Estes' value as a slave. The first number was larger.

"I want you to go to California with my boys," Mr. Estes said to Howard the next day. "But how do I know you'll come back? You might find gold and decide to run."

"My family is here." Howard replied. "I would never leave them." Mr. Estes knew that this was true. Howard Estes was a family man.

After Mr. Estes agreed to send him to California, Howard began talking about all the money he could make gold mining. Before long, he planted the idea in Mr. Estes' head that he could make money by letting Howard work in California for awhile.

In the end, Mr. Estes told Sylvia's father that he could stay in California and work in a gold mine. He said that Howard could keep some of the money he earned there. Mr. Estes promised to sell Howard his freedom papers for $1,000. This was just what Howard had been planning.

Bought Out of Slavery

Howard Estes was gone from his family for almost two years. It was a long, hard wait for Hannah Estes. Sylvia watched her mother go to a shed behind the house every day. Sylvia followed her one day and looked in through a crack. Hannah Estes was kneeling, praying for her husband to come home safely. She also prayed that her children would be free.

Howard Estes worked in a gold mine in California. He saved all the money he earned. In a few months he saved $1,000 and sent it to his master, but Mr. Estes refused to give Howard his freedom papers.

When Hannah's master, Mr. Leopold, found out that Mr. Estes had broken his promise to Howard, Mr. Leopold offered to help. Howard Estes sent another $1,000 to Mr. Leopold so that Mr. Leopold could buy Howard's freedom papers from Mr. Estes.

Finally, Mr. Estes agreed to sell Howard's papers to Mr. Leopold. Mr. Leopold sent Howard's freedom papers to him in California. When Howard received them, he sewed a small leather purse so that he could carry his papers with him all the time.

Howard Estes stayed in California until he had enough money to buy his whole family out of slavery.

During the two years that Howard Estes was away, Sylvia's sister Agnes died of scarlet fever. Just before she died, Agnes told Sylvia about the dream she had the night before. She dreamt that her father was walking towards her through a meadow. He was wearing a new grey suit, a white panama hat and a tie of many colors.

A year later, Agnes' dream came true. Sylvia saw her father coming towards her through the meadow. He was wearing a grey suit, a white hat and a colorful tie. He had a carpet bag and a coat over his arm.

The Estes family was together again. They were not slaves anymore. But it would be a long time before they would be free from fear and racism.

Howard Estes paid Mr. Leopold $1,000 each for Hannah Estes and Sylvia's brother Jackson. He paid $900 for Sylvia.

"Sure Mr. Leopold helped us," Hannah Estes said, "but he made a whole lot of money, too!"

Sylvia's parents bought a farm in Missouri. The family lived and worked together for the first time. They grew vegetables, raised chickens and sold eggs. But although they were not slaves, they were still not safe.

Many nights Sylvia feared for her life. Sometimes strange men surrounded the house and threatened to burn it down. Sylvia and her family hid in the dark house until the men went away. Other free African-Americans were beaten and kidnapped. Howard and Hannah Estes wanted to leave Missouri as soon as possible.

CHAPTER THREE

Moving to California

Wagon Train to California

Hannah's old master, Charles Leopold, decided to take a herd of cattle to California to sell. He hired Sylvia's father, her brother Jackson and some other men to help him. Mr. Leopold hired Hannah Estes to cook.

Mr. Leopold gave Howard Estes a covered wagon with a broken axle. Howard fixed the axle, and he and Hannah made the wagon into a home for their family. On April 1, 1851, Hannah, Howard and their children left Missouri with Mr. Leopold and a small caravan of covered wagons and cattle.

The Leopold caravan was small. Some of the caravans traveling to California on the Oregon Trail were a mile long and a mile wide. The wagons churned up huge plumes of dust that surrounded the caravan like smoke from a fire. The caravans would spread out so the wagon drivers could breathe and see where they were going.

Sylvia crossed hundreds of miles of flat land, called plains, in what are now the states of Nebraska and Wyoming. She liked the little prairie dogs that popped up from their underground homes. The caravan passed enormous herds of bison, commonly called buffalo, that stampeded when they saw the wagons. There were beautiful flowers on the plains, and locusts and mosquitoes, too. There were so many mosquitoes that they completely covered the lids of the pots while Hannah Estes was cooking.

Plains Indian Tribes

Many different tribes, or nations, of American Indians lived on the plains. During the first months of their trip, the Estes traveled through land where the Kansa and Pawne tribes lived and hunted. The people of these tribes believed that land could not be owned. To them, all beings were equal and all shared the land, sky and water.

Sylvia saw wagons piled high with bison hides headed toward California on the trail. White hunters skinned bison and sold the hides for lots of money in California. Sylvia saw the bison carcasses the white hunters had left behind, rotting on the ground.

When the Plains Indians killed bison, they used all parts of the animal. They ate the meat and they used the horns to make cups and bowls. They used bison skulls for decoration, and bones for stakes for their teepees. They even used bison brains to cure the bisons' hide. When the jelly-like brains were rubbed into a dried hide, it became supple and waterproof. When white hunters took only bison hides and left everything else to rot, the Plains Indians were angry.

This was one of the reasons the Kansa or Pawne warriors sometimes attacked caravans that passed through their hunting territory. Warriors sometimes took cattle and horses from the caravans.

A Close Call

One afternoon, the Estes' caravan made camp early to let the cattle rest and graze. Suddenly, a band of warriors on horses surrounded the camp. They tried to make the cattle stampede, but the cattle were too tired to run.

Charles Leopold and the other herders ran to get their guns, but Howard Estes cried out.

"No! Wait!" Howard yelled. "We are outnumbered. The only way for us to stay alive is to talk with them." The other herders did not know what to do. They looked at Mr. Leopold. Mr. Leopold trusted Howard's judgment. He knew Howard wanted to protect his family.

Howard Estes and Mr. Leopold put down their guns and walked towards the warriors. They went to the chief's tent. The chief spoke English. They gave the chief gifts of flour and other food and also three horses.

The chief accepted the gifts. He went to the door of his tent and gave one loud whoop. All the other warriors instantly stopped shouting and left.

A Visit With the Mormons

Sylvia's family and the caravan arrived in Salt Lake City, Utah, at harvest time. They stayed for a week to rest the cattle and buy more supplies.

Salt Lake City was founded by Brigham Young and his followers in the Mormon Church. Mormons came from all over North America to live in Salt Lake City. Some of the first settlers were too poor to buy a horse and wagon. They carried their belongings hundreds of miles in wheelbarrows.

The Mormons had their own laws. Sylvia learned a little about those laws during her stay in Salt Lake City.

One day a Mormon woman came to visit Hannah Estes. The woman was upset. Hannah gave her a cup of water. Sylvia sat with the women and listened while the Mormon woman told Hannah her problem.

"I don't know what to do," the woman said. "The church fathers told my husband to get another wife or leave Salt Lake City. But we spent all our money getting here. So he married an Indian. She lives next to us and now they have a child." The woman started to cry.

"I don't want to share my husband, but there is nothing I can do," said the woman as she left.

"These Mormons think a husband is the master," Hannah Estes told her husband later. "I've had enough of masters. This is not the place for me!"

California! A New Home

The caravan arrived in Sacramento, California, on November 3, 1851. They had been traveling for six months and three days. The caravan broke up. Mr. Leopold sold his cattle and went home to Missouri.

Maybe Hannah and Howard Estes were sorry to say goodbye to Mr. Leopold because he had helped them to freedom. Maybe they were happy to be rid of a man who had held them as slaves. When Sylvia Stark told her daughter Marie about this years later, she did not tell Marie how she felt. The Estes never saw Mr. Leopold again. That chapter of their lives was over.

Sylvia and her family went to a gold mining area sixty miles from Sacramento. They found an empty miner's cabin near a town called Placerville.

It did not take long to move their belongings into the cabin. Sylvia found a cooking pot. She and Jackson gathered twigs to make a fire. Howard Estes went to the store with his last dollar to buy some meat.

When Howard put the ham on the counter, the storekeeper looked at Howard's face.

"You're new here, aren't you?" the storekeeper said. Howard nodded, fearful of what the man would say next.

"You have an honest face and we need more honest people here in Placerville." The storekeeper put some flour, tea, baking soda and a cabbage on the counter next to the ham. "These groceries are on the house."

Howard thanked him for his kindness.

"That was one time my face was of value," Howard said to Hannah when he brought her the food.

The Estes ate ham and cabbage and dumplings that night. After they had eaten, Hannah told her family,

"We will have to work hard, but we're welcome here and we are working for ourselves."

CHAPTER FOUR

Life Is Dangerous

Life in California

Sylvia and her family lived a few miles from Placerville. Sylvia was glad they did not live in town because Placerville was a rough place. There was no sheriff. Many people came and went, looking for gold. If a person found gold, he or she suddenly had a lot of money. People were often robbed, and sometimes murdered. Sylvia and her family slept with their cabin tightly locked, even in the summer.

The Estes family had a small farm. They grew grain which was ground into flour at a mill. They also grew fruit and vegetables. During good years, they had enough fruit and vegetables to give away. Sylvia took care of the chickens and collected eggs. The Estes kept cows as well, and sold butter in Placerville.

Howard Estes worked in a gold mine. Sylvia and Jackson panned for gold in rivers near old mines. They sold gold dust and earned about a dollar a day.

Hannah Estes took in washing. She charged $3.00 to wash and iron a pleated skirt, and $5.00 for a frilled dress. Sylvia helped her mother with the washing. While Hannah ironed the clothes, Sylvia rubbed her mother's shoulders with a warm iron to ease her rheumatism.

Sylvia loved to walk along the trails in the hills near the cabin. She and Jackson explored the country-side together. Sylvia liked to pick the yellow poppies and red geraniums that grew wild. There were rattlesnakes up in the hills. Sylvia learned to walk away when she heard the rattle, but Hannah Estes killed snakes with stones. A rattlesnake bite could kill a person if help was not received right away.

Miwok Neighbors

Miwok Indians lived around Placerville. The Miwok lived on plants they gathered. They also fished and hunted small animals. The Miwok did not live in tepees like the Plains tribes. They built houses out of wood pole frames, which they covered with grass or palm fronds or leaves. The Miwok wove beautiful baskets.

When miners came to find gold, they took over Miwok land. The Miwok moved aside to make room for the new-comers. They were not warriors like the Pawnee or the Kansa. Many Miwok died from diseases like smallpox that the miners brought with them to California.

Sylvia and Jackson visited with nearby Miwok and learned some of their customs. For example, they made bread out of pounded acorn nuts. Roasted grasshoppers were a special treat for the Miwok. They drove the grass-hoppers into the hot embers of a fire to cook them.

An old Miwok woman lived near the Estes cabin. She had no money. Hannah Estes always gave her a meal when the woman came to their door. Hannah also gave her fruit or vegetables to take home.

A Visit and a Story of Trouble

One day a white man came to the Estes cabin and asked Howard Estes for help. The man wanted to borrow the Estes' horse and wagon. "My wife and children are waiting for me on the highway," the man said. "I have to fetch them."

The man's wife and children had come across the plains to join him in California. After months of travel, they were almost to their new home. The man had asked all the other neighbors to lend him a horse and wagon but no one would. He was asking Black people for a favor as a last resort.

Howard Estes wanted to trust the man but he could not afford to lose his wagon. Howard asked Hannah for her opinion. Hannah Estes looked hard at the man. She was a good judge of character. She could see that he was telling the truth. The Estes gave him the horse and wagon, and then waited for him. Time passed.

The man finally returned after dark with his wife and children. His wife wanted to meet Hannah Estes. Sylvia listened while she told Hannah about her journey to California. This is what she said:

The woman left her home state of Arkansas with her two little children. Her husband was waiting for them in in their new California home. She joined a caravan owned by a man she knew and trusted. But, unlike Hannah Estes, she was not a good judge of character.

The man waited until they were away from all towns and then told her that she had to give him her money and her wedding ring to pay for food. "No!" she said. He threatened to leave her and her children on the side of the trail. She still said, "No!" The man kicked her and her children out and left them on the empty plain.

They had no food and no place to sleep. The woman was afraid of wolves and Indians, and afraid of being alone in the dark. "We'll starve to death," she thought.

Night was coming and she held her children to protect them. Then she saw two men coming toward her. They were walking with a mule. The mule had big packs on its back. When they came closer, she saw that they were Black men. One was tall and wore a hat. The other had a long beard.

Growing up in Arkansas, she had been taught not to trust Black people, but now she needed help. She told them her story.

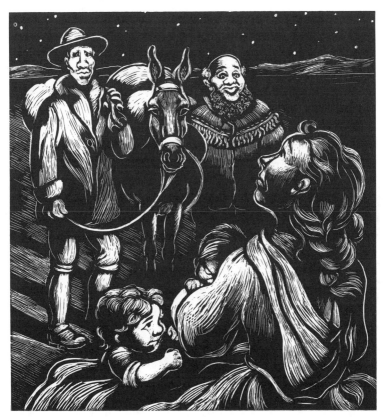

"What can we do?" the tall man said to the other. "We don't have enough food for ourselves."

"But we can't leave her," said the man with the beard.

"No, we can't," the tall man agreed.

"Can you walk?" the man with the beard asked. He looked sorry for her. She said she could. "Well, put the children on the mule," he told her.

The two men hardly ate so that there was enough food for the children. In a few days they came to a settlement of white people.

"Now you are with your own people," the bearded man said. "They will take care of you."

"You have taken better care of us than my own people did," the woman said, taking each of them by the hand. "I have no money or anything to give you. All I can say is thank you and God bless you." The men bought supplies and headed out toward the setting sun. The woman soon joined another caravan and she and her children finished the trip to California safely.

After the woman told her story to Hannah, she was quiet for a moment. Sylvia thought about the wolves howling out on the plains, and moved closer to her mother. The woman sighed and said to Hannah, "I have nothing to give you, either, Mrs. Estes, but God bless you for trusting my husband and helping us in a time of need."

• • • • •

Sylvia Marries Louis Stark

When Sylvia was fifteen she met Louis Stark. Louis was a strong, handsome man with a quick temper. He owned a dairy farm near Placerville. Louis was about thirty years old. He had traveled a lot and worked many different jobs.

Louis Stark was born in Kentucky. His mother was African-American and his father was white. Louis's mother was a slave on the plantation owned by his father. Louis's skin was light and his hair was dark and wavy. Louis's coloring helped him. He could pass for white and because of this, Louis was able to go places and buy things other Black people could not.

Louis Stark was not a slave. His father taught Louis to be a foreman on his plantation. As a young man, Louis carried a whip. He learned to force other people to obey him. People said this was why he was so bad-tempered.

Louis had many skills. On his father's plantation he learned about growing and grafting fruit trees. When he quit the plantation, he became a barber on river boats that traveled up and down the Mississippi River.

Not long after Louis and Sylvia met, Louis wanted to marry Sylvia. Hannah Estes was against the marriage. She did not like Louis Stark.

"He's too old," Hannah told Sylvia. "He does not believe in God. And he has a mean streak a mile wide."

But Louis knew how to get what he wanted. He kept courting Sylvia. He talked about the farm they would buy and the garden he would make her.

Sylvia thought that Louis was sweet and very handsome. But there was something else that made her decide to marry him. Louis did not think, talk or act like a slave. He believed he could do anything, and Sylvia admired him for it.

Louis and Sylvia were married in September 1855. Sylvia was sixteen years old.

Sylvia left her parent's cabin and went to live with Louis. Soon she missed her family. Louis was hard to live with. He was moody. After three weeks, Sylvia wanted to go home to her parents, but Louis persuaded her to stay.

Sylvia stayed with Louis for many years. They often disagreed but Sylvia and Louis had the same dream: to live and farm on their own land. Together, they worked hard to make their dream come true.

• • • • •

Time to Move On

Sylvia and Louis visited with Sylvia's parents every Sunday afternoon. Louis and Howard Estes talked about their crops while Sylvia visited with her mother in the kitchen. But when they sat down to dinner, they always talked about the same subject: California was becoming a dangerous place for them to live.

A few years after Sylvia and Louis were married, Howard and Hannah Estes began talking about leaving California. Howard did not want to leave his farm and the fruit trees he had planted.

"How can we leave our friends and our church?" he said to Sylvia and Louis one evening after dinner. "And leave this farm, after clearing all those rocks from the fields and digging that deep well?" But Hannah insisted that they must leave.

"We came here to be left alone and these people won't let us be," Hannah said angrily. Hannah stood with her hands on her hips while Howard shook his head. Sylvia remembered how angry her mother used to get at Mrs. Leopold when Mrs. Leopold called her "nigger."

"What about the Robinsons, down the road?" Hannah continued. "Mr. Robinson went to the store and Mrs. Robinson never saw him again. A slave trader picked him up. And the Spotts, over on the other side of Placerville? A white man showed up at the Spotts' farm and said he owned it now. There was nothing they could do, after farming it for all those years. We have to leave this place before I lose Howard, or we lose the farm."

Sylvia and Louis agreed with Hannah. They decided to leave California with Sylvia's parents. Many other African-Americans also wanted to leave. These people knew that the freedom they had hoped to find in California was not a reality. It was time to move on.

CHAPTER FIVE

A Meeting at Zion

Dangerous Laws

California became a state in 1850. Slavery was illegal in this new state, but there were laws that threatened the lives and property of the Estes and the Starks and all African-Americans.

A California law called the 1850 Civil Practice Act said that no Black person could testify against a white person in court. This meant that homesteaders like the Estes, and their neighbors the Spotts, could not testify in court to protect their land if a white man claimed it.

A federal law called the Fugitive Slave Act said that slave owners could recapture slaves who had escaped to free states, where slavery was illegal. This meant that any Black person could be kidnapped and taken back to the South and sold.

Many people, like the Estes, had freedom papers that said they were freed from slavery. This should have protected them, but if they could not testify in court, how could they prove that they were free?

And then, in 1857, the United States Supreme Court ruled that people of African descent were not American citizens. This was called the Dred Scott Decision. It did not matter if the person was free or in slavery. Black people had no rights and they were not protected by the United States Constitution.

Many Black people in California owned property. Some had become rich by opening business and working hard. These people paid taxes, but they could not vote. They got together to decide what they should do.

Zion Church Meeting

On April 14, 1858, about six hundred Black people met at the Zion Methodist Episcopal Church in San Francisco. The church was filled. Many people crowded around outside to catch the first news of what was going on inside. Inside and out, men and women were telling each other, "We can't live here any more. Where can we go? Where can we be free and live in peace?"

Inside the church, a white man stood up to talk. People grew quiet as the man held up a map and started talking about rich farmland and gold on an island called Vancouver Island, far to the north.

Douglas's letter

The white man was the captain of a steamship that sailed between San Francisco and Fort Victoria, on Vancouver Island. After he talked about the good farmland around Victoria, he read a letter from Governor James Douglas of Victoria. Douglas was the Governor of New Caledonia, a British Colony made up of Vancouver Island and the small surrounding islands.

Governor Douglas's letter invited the Black people of California to move to his colony and become citizens of the colony. He promised that they would not be discriminated against on the basis of race.

Douglas wanted African-Americans to come to Victoria because the city needed honest, hard-working people. There was a gold rush in the Fraser River valley, north of Victoria. Gold miners sailed to Victoria on their way to the mines. They needed food, clothes and tools. They needed places to stay and restaurants to eat in. Victoria was a good place to start a business or run a farm.

The people at the Zion Church meeting discussed the letter. Was Captain Nagle telling the truth about Victoria, or did he just want passengers for his ship? Would Black people be free in Vancouver, or was Governor Douglas making promises to get skilled workers for Victoria and Vancouver Island? They decided to send a delegation up to Victoria to see for themselves.

The Pioneer Committee

Two weeks after the meeting at Zion Church, thirty-five African-Americans sailed up to Victoria. They were the "Pioneer Committee." They would find out about Victoria and report back to San Francisco.

Victoria was a busy town. All along the muddy streets, there were tiny shops. There were many small hotels and bars. The first thing the Pioneer Committee did in Victoria was rent a room for a prayer meeting. Then they got to work.

Within one week, some people from the Pioneer Committee bought land in Victoria. Others started a brick-making company. Many began working on farms outside of town and some joined the police force in Victoria.

Three men from the Pioneer Committee met with Governor Douglas. They were surprised to see he was a dark-skinned man. His mother was a Black woman from the West Indies. Perhaps they would be treated fairly by Governor Douglas!

Land cost a lot of money on Vancouver Island, but Governor Douglas offered a deal.

Governor Douglas said that there was a lot of land in the colony that the government had not surveyed. He offered this land to new settlers for less money. The new settlers would pay twenty-five percent of the price at first and the remainder over four years. They didn't have to pay taxes for two years.

Best of all, Douglas promised that anyone who owned land could vote.

One man from the Pioneer Committee returned to San Francisco with good news. He spoke to a meeting of 350 people at Zion Church. He told them about Douglas's promise and he read them a letter from Wellington Moses, another man on the Pioneer Committee. Moses wrote: "Victoria is a God-sent land for our people."

People at the Zion meeting talked about many subjects. They wrote them down so that people in the future would know what they thought and felt.

Some people at the meeting wrote that they were angry with the United States. The U.S. was their home but they were treated like slaves. Other people wrote

"We thank Governor Douglas for his invitation." Everybody thanked the Pioneer Committee. Many people wrote down business advice.

The people at the meeting also made an important decision. They decided it would be better to integrate with white people in Victoria, in the schools, churches and socially, than to create a separate Black community.

It was an exciting time for the Black community in northern California. It was also a sad time. Farmers like Howard Estes sold their farms. Business people in San Francisco sold their shops. People who were leaving had to say goodbye to friends and family who were staying in California.

Sylvia Stark did not have to leave her family. Her parents and her brother Jackson also wanted to farm on Vancouver Island. Sylvia and Louis decided to move with their two young children. Once again, Sylvia was leaving her home and moving to a strange, new place.

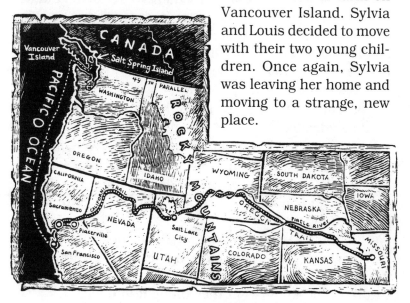

CHAPTER SIX

A New Country

Sailing Up the Coast

During the spring and summer of 1858, about six hundred African-Americans emigrated from California to Vancouver Island. Louis Stark sold all but fifty of his cows. Sylvia and Louis packed up their belongings. With the two small children, Willis and Emma,they had so much to do.

Most people who left California for Victoria went by steamship. Sylvia traveled up the coast on a ship called the *Brother Jonathan* with her parents and her children.

Louis Stark and Sylvia's brother Jackson traveled overland. Louis wanted to take his cattle, and fifty was too many to bring on a boat.

The *Brother Jonathan* was an old boat. It was not seaworthy. As they sailed up the coast of Oregon, the ocean swells got bigger and bigger. The boat creaked and groaned. Sylvia was frightened.

"Throw the horses overboard!" the captain ordered. Forty horses were brought to the deck from the cargo hold of the boat and thrown overboard. Sylvia told her daughter later how sad she was to hear the horses cry and to see them swimming helplessly after the boat.

The *Brother Jonathan* finally made it to Steilacoom, in Washington Territory. Sylvia and her family waited there for a month until Louis and Jackson arrived with the cattle.

When Louis and Jackson arrived, the family sailed to Victoria with the cattle aboard the ship. There were no storms on this part of the trip. Soon they were sailing into the protected harbor of Victoria.

Victoria

The sun was shining in the town of Fort Victoria. The mud from the winter rain had dried and flowers were blooming. Sylvia and her family walked along the wooden sidewalks. Emma and Willis held onto their mother as they walked past large rough-wood buildings. The smell of fresh-cut wood was everywhere. They passed a trading post and sniffed the sour smell of bundled pelts. There were people everywhere.

Sylvia saw many different kinds of people. Most of them were men. Some were Black and some were white. There were also Asians and people from the South Pacific Islands.

Men and women from Indian tribes were camped on the outskirts of town. They were Haida, Cowichan, Bella Bella, Kwakiutl and Coast Salish Indians. They came to Victoria from as far away as the Queen Charlotte Islands to sell and trade.

Louis stopped a Black man on the street and asked where they could find a hotel. Soon all seven members of Sylvia's family were squeezed into the only hotel room available.

The next day Louis Stark secured naturalization papers for his family so they could all become citizens of the British colony. Now they needed to buy land.

Hannah and Howard Estes bought farmland in Saanich, near Victoria. Louis and Sylvia Stark did not have enough money to buy land. They decided to settle on Salt Spring Island.

Salt Spring was a large island close to Vancouver Island. It was named for a ground spring on the island where salt water bubbled up. People were just beginning to homestead land on Salt Spring Island.

During the summer months, Howard Estes helped Louis Stark clear land and build a cabin on Salt Spring Island. Sylvia, Jackson and Hannah Estes stayed in Saanich. Sylvia took care of Willis and Emma, helped her mother in the garden and tended the cattle.

A Scary Welcome to Salt Spring Island

Sylvia and her children moved to Salt Spring Island on a sunny summer day in 1860. Louis came to Fort Victoria and together the family sailed from Victoria to Salt Spring. They brought everything for their new home with them in trunks. They had plates and pots, blankets and a few chairs, a butter churn and even an iron. All of their cattle were on the boat as well.

The boat dropped anchor in the middle of a small bay, called Vesuvius Bay, on Salt Spring Island. There was no dock on the island, so the cattle were lowered into the water by ropes. They swam to land and quickly found the trail through the woods to their new home.

A Cowichan woman and man each paddled a canoe from the shore to meet the Starks. Sylvia and the children got into one canoe and Louis piled their belongings into the other.

When they landed on the shore, a white man greeted them and helped unload the boats. His name was McCauly. He did not live on Salt Spring but he knew Louis and had come to help. Sylvia and the children waited on the beach with the Cowichans and McCauly. Louis went to get a wheelbarrow.

Suddenly, seven canoes came into the bay. "Haidas!" said the Cowichan woman. She looked frightened. Sylvia called out to Emma and Willis. She knew the Haidas were hunters and warriors. They had paddled down from the Queen Charlotte Islands, far to the north. Haidas and Cowichans were enemies.

The Cowichan woman slipped away to get help from her village as the seven canoes pulled onto the beach.

The Haidas looked at all the things in the Starks' trunks, while the Cowichan man sat quietly on the beach. McCauly, the white man, spoke to the Haidas in their language.

Suddenly, one of the Haidas pulled out a knife and held it to McCauly's throat. Sylvia gasped in surprise and fear. She could see that McCauly was trembling, but he kept talking until the Haida put the knife away.

Clutching Willis and Emma tightly, Sylvia watched the Haidas leave the trunks and gather around McCauly. McCauly argued with them for a few minutes and then, abruptly, he and the Haida's got into the canoes and left.

When the Cowichan woman reached her village, she warned her people of the Haidas' arrival. Cowichan warriors set out to find the Haidas. Later that day, in the water just east of Salt Spring Island, there was a bloodly battle between the Cowichan and the Haidas.

"McCauly told us later that he was pretty sure the Haidas wouldn't hurt him. He went with them to get them away from us and our trunks," Sylvia told her daughter Marie years later. "He was just lucky that he wasn't in the Haidas' canoes when the Cowichans found them.

"That was my welcome to the island," Sylvia told Marie. "Scared me half to death. It was a month before I'd let the children out of my sight."

The New Home

Sylvia was still in shock when she saw her new home. It was a log cabin with no roof or door. Trees and thick bushes grew right up to it. Louis Stark had worked hard to build it, but there was much more work to do.

Sylvia sat on a log, holding her head in her hands. The fear she had felt on the beach was ebbing away, but she was still trembling. She was six months pregnant and her baby kicked inside her. Sylvia felt tired and discouraged. It seemed that no matter where she went, there was always someone threatening to hurt her and her family. She longed for comfort and safety.

"Sylvia, come here," Louis called from the cabin. "Come see your new house."

Sylvia walked slowly to the cabin. The inside was rough but Louis had made a beautiful bed frame out of bent saplings and covered it with her favorite quilt.

"Don't worry," Louis said, putting his arm around her. "Things will get better."

CHAPTER SEVEN

Living on a Wilderness Island

Settling on Salt Spring Island

In 1860, Salt Spring Island was a wilderness island. Cougars, bears and a few wolves lived and hunted on the island. Sylvia could hear the mewing of baby cougars from the porch of her new home. Full-grown cougars stole chickens and terrorized the other farm animals.

Nobody had lived on Salt Spring before the Starks and other farmers began settling the island. The steep hills and dense forest made even walking difficult. Cowichan and Haida Indians visited Salt Spring to hunt, and most of them were friendly. The Cowichan sold salmon and berries to the settlers.

Louis Stark used the skills and knowledge he had learned in Kentucky to make a farm in the Salt Spring wilderness. He felled trees around the cabin and split them into rails for fencing. The first year on the island, he cut and dried wild meadow grass for the cattle. The next year he cleared a meadow and planted it.

Louis tilled the meadow with a plough he made out of a V-shaped tree. He put a blade at the bottom of the V and spikes along the sides. A pair of oxen pulled it.

Louis and Sylvia grew turnips and bran to feed the cattle. They had beef cattle and dairy cows. They also raised chickens, turkeys and pigs. Sylvia fed her family year-round with the food she grew in her garden.

The children, Willis and Emma, and John, who was born soon after the family arrived on Salt Spring, went to school on the island. The school was a log cabin at the crossroads at the center of the island. The teacher, John Craven Jones, was a Black man from Ohio. He had moved to Salt Spring with his two brothers after he graduated from Oberlin College in Ohio.

John Craven Jones taught all the children on Salt Spring for many years without being paid in money. People gave him food and a place to live.

Comfort in Prayer

The early years on Salt Spring were lonely for Sylvia. The Stark's cabin was separated from other settlers at Vesuvius Bay by thick forest. Sometimes Sylvia did not see her neighbors for weeks.

Sylvia was separated from her parents and her brother for the first time. There were no women to give her advice about raising her children. Louis often went to Victoria to buy provisions or do business, and Sylvia was alone for days or weeks.

It was at this time that Sylvia found comfort in prayer. Years later she told her daughter Marie, "Now I can see the hand of God guiding me through all of my troubles, guiding me to a higher life."

Louis Stark was not religious. He did not like to see his wife praying. When Louis was home, Sylvia snuck into the woods to pray. She was not afraid of the cougars then. She remembered her mother praying in the shed in Missouri. Sylvia kept in her heart the words from the Bible: "Fear not for I am with thee."

Uninvited Visitors

The nearby Cowichan Indians helped the settlers of Salt Spring Island in many ways. They carried people and their belongings between the island and the mainland in their canoes. They traded food with the settlers and taught them about the plants on the island. They showed settlers how to dry or cure fish, deer and other game.

Most of the local Indians and most of the settlers were friendly with each other. But a few individual Cowichan and Haidas did not want farmers on their hunting ground. They believed they had a right to anything they found on the island. When they came to Salt Spring to hunt, they took the settlers' chickens and raided their gardens.

Several settlers were killed by Indians during the first five years the Starks lived on Salt Spring. Two settlers were killed at Vesuvius Bay, near the Starks' land. The Starks came close to being hurt or killed by Indians many times.

One Sunday evening Sylvia, Louis and their children were sitting in their cabin. Suddenly, five Indians walked in and began looking at and touching everything in the house. One man took down a gun from the fireplace mantle.

"Be careful!" Louis Stark shouted. "It's loaded!" He grabbed the muzzle to turn it towards the ceiling.

Louis and the other man struggled. Sylvia prayed while she watched. She knew the men had come to kill them. The Starks were outnumbered.

While the two men fought, the gun went off. It shot a hole in the roof. The Indian man let go. The Indians left quickly because Stark was holding the gun. They knew he was a good shot.

After the Indians left, Sylvia calmed the children, but she was still trembling as she got ready for bed. "Why did you ever bring us to this place," she said to Louis angrily. "We would be dead if you hadn't been here." Louis said nothing. He had often told her not to worry about the Indians, but tonight he could not argue. They had all been in serious danger.

Leaving Vesuvius Bay

After the Indian attack, Louis agreed that Sylvia was right. Life at Vesuvius Bay was too dangerous. Louis did not want to leave the land he had cleared and cultivated, but he couldn't hire anyone to help him bring in his crops. Louis and Sylvia traveled around Salt Spring looking for good land. They decided to move to Fruitville, an area on the east side of Salt Spring Island.

The Stark's new homestead was on a bigger bay, with a beach. Louis spent two months clearing land and putting up a lean-to for the family to live in while he built a house. The day they moved into the lean-to, Sylvia and the children went to the beach to collect clams and mussels from the shore. As they sat outside the lean-to eating clams that evening, they could hear whales blowing in the bay. Sylvia took a deep breath and smiled.

"Finally," she thought, "I feel safe. This is my home."

CHAPTER EIGHT

Leaving
Salt Spring Island

A New Farm

Louis spent most of the spring and summer of 1868 working on the new house at Fruitville. Howard Estes came over from Saanich to help, while Willis took care of ploughing and planting the new farm. Sylvia was thrilled with her new house. It had three bedrooms and a large kitchen. The Stark family had grown bigger. When they moved into the house, Sylvia and Louis had six children: Willis, Emma, John, Abraham, Serena and Marie. Abraham was a sickly and usually stayed inside.

"You have always lived in cabins," Sylvia told her children. "Now we're going to live in a real house, with a real floor and lots of rooms."

After they moved into the house, Sylvia and Louis let a new family stay in the lean-to until they cleared land for a house of their own. Their name was Frederson and they were from Hawaii. Sylvia enjoyed having the Fredersons as neighbors. Emma, Serena and Marie like to visit Mrs. Frederson and help her bake cookies.

Sylvia was happy on their new farm. Her garden was close to the house, and the sheep and cows grazed nearby. Her younger children loved to explore the beach.

"I don't want to move ever again," she declared.

Louis spent more and more of his time in the town of Cedar on Vancouver Island, where he mined for minerals. Sylvia and Louis' oldest son Willis ran the farm. Willis was sixteen years old and he planned to spend his life on Salt Spring Island. He was already famous on the island as a cougar hunter.

Sylvia's second son, John, was only fourteen but he was ready to leave the island. He wanted to travel up north to explore and prospect for minerals like his father.

Leaving Salt Spring Island

Sylvia loved the Fruitville farm, but Louis wasn't happy. He wanted to move the family to Cedar, on Vancouver Island. Louis was tired of farming. "There is money in those mineral mines, just waiting to be taken," he told Sylvia. "If we stay here, we'll always be poor."

Louis worked in Cedar mining for minerals for weeks or months at a time. Sylvia lived with the children on Salt Spring.

Life was easier when Louis was not around because there was no fighting. But Sylvia believed a wife should stay with her husband. Finally, she agreed to move to Cedar. Louis bought a house there and built an addition.

Sylvia left Salt Spring in the fall of 1874 with three of her children: Abraham, age eleven, Serena, age nine, and Marie, age seven. Willis stayed on the island to run the farm. John left to begin his life of travel and adventure.

The oldest daughter, Emma, also stayed on Salt Spring. She taught school on the island for three years.

Sylvia and the children sailed to Nanaimo on a sturdy tugboat named *The Maud*. A light snow fell on the water and the rocks along the shore as the boat pulled up to the dock in Cedar. Sylvia shivered and thought about the cozy home she was leaving. It is too quiet here, she thought. It did not feel like a good place to Sylvia.

Two young boys watched the tugboat from the dock. Serena put her hand in Sylvia's hand. Then she waved to the boys. They waved back.

"She is the same age I was when we left Missouri," Sylvia thought. Sylvia remembered being on the wagon train when she was a girl. She recalled playing tag with the other children, and running between wagons and hiding in the dust. Sylvia was thirty-five years old but she felt very old.

Starting a new farm was easier with children to help. The children collected firewood, fed the animals, churned butter and weeded the garden. Sylvia taught Serena to spin. The children learned to read and write in school.

Two years after moving to Cedar, Sylvia gave birth to her last child. Louis and Sylvia named her Louisa. She was much younger than her brothers and sisters.

Louis Stark had been working so hard to feed and protect his family when his other children were born that he didn't have time to pay much attention to them. Louis had time for this baby. He took care of Louisa in the evenings and on Sundays, when Sylvia went to church. He brought her with him when he went to Victoria to buy supplies. It seemed that Louis and Louisa were always together.

Living Her Own Life on Salt Spring Island

Sylvia missed the Fruitville farm and she did not like Cedar. Her neighbors were miners, not farmers. She found few friends. She went to the small wooden church on Sundays, but the minister had a face like a lemon. Sylvia did not like his sour sermons.

Louis traveled up and down the coast, prospecting for gold and minerals. He was gone from Cedar for weeks at a time. When Louis was at home, sometimes he bossed Sylvia around. Other times he did not talk to her at all. Sylvia had hoped that moving to Cedar would end the fights between Louis and her. But they still could not get along. It seemed to Sylvia that she and Louis could not say two words to each other without having an argument.

One day when Louis returned home from a trip up north, Sylvia had her bags packed. She told Louis that she was going back to Fruitville. "I don't care if I'm poor," she told him. "Fruitville is my home, where my church and friends are."

The older children were glad to go back to Salt Spring Island, but Louisa had never been there. Louisa did not want to leave her mother, but she clung to her father. Louis and Sylvia argued, but in the end Sylvia agreed to leave Louisa.

On the boat back to Salt Spring, Sylvia cried for the loss of her daughter. She also missed Louis for many years, but she knew that she could not give up her happiness for him. After watching him stand up for himself for so many years, she knew she had to stand up for herself. Now Sylvia was on her own.

CHAPTER NINE

Return to Salt Spring

A Long Life on Salt Spring Island

Sylvia was forty-six years old when she moved back to Salt Spring. Her travels ended but her life continued. For the next fifty-nine years Sylvia Stark lived with her son Willis on the island. They raised pigs and goats, kept a few cows and many chickens. Sylvia traded eggs for groceries at the central store and preserved vegetables from her garden to eat all year.

Willis drove his mother to church every Sunday in his horse drawn wagon. Sylvia often brought food and herbs to friends and neighbors who were ill. Sylvia was respected by everyone on the island.

When Sylvia and Willis needed help, they hired people to hay their fields and cut and stack wood. Sylvia used to joke that every man on the Island had worked for her. Sylvia cleared and planted her small garden even when she was 100 years old.

As Sylvia and Willis grew older, the land that Willis had cleared for the farm became smaller. Every spring, brambles and sapling trees sprung up in the meadows. Willis and a neighbor cut them back, but the forest pressed in and the fields shrunk.

Sylvia Stark and Willis lived together until Willis died in 1943, at the age of eighty-five. Sylvia lived for one more year. She died in November, 1944, at the age of 105. She was independent until her death. She would not move out of her house, even when she needed a lot of help.

All of Sylvia and Louis Stark's children except Willis left Salt Spring Island. They moved to the cities of Victoria and Vancouver, in British Columbia. Their children and grandchildren spread out over Canada and the United States.

Sylvia Stark's Granddaughters

When Ernie and I visited Sylvia Stark's grand-daughter Ethel Claibourne at the old farm, the fruit trees were old and gnarled. A narrow meadow sloped up behind the house, with tall trees and thick bushes all around. Two cats watched us from the front porch as we came through the gate. Inside the house, the low ceilings and thick walls kept the chill of the rainy outdoors away.

Mrs. Claibourne and her husband had raised their children in California. When the children were grown, the Claibournes moved back to Salt Spring Island. Mrs. Claibourne lives today with her daughter Yvonne on Salt Spring in Sylvia's old house. Mrs. Claibourne's sister Myrtle Holloman also returned to Salt Spring after many years of living in the United States.

Like most people, Mrs. Claibourne and Mrs. Holloman would rather talk about their children and grandchildren than their grandmother. Mrs. Claibourne showed us a picture of the newest baby in her family.

"I have great-great-grandchildren," Mrs. Claibourne told us. "There is German, Italian, English and Mexican blood in the family now."

Mrs. Claibourne and her sister Myrtle Holloman showed us photographs of members of their family, from their great-grandfather, Howard Estes, taken in the 1860s, to Mrs. Claibourne's great-great-grandson, born in 1990. He is a lucky baby. When he grows up, he will hear stories about his family from six generations before he was born.

One Last Visit to The Ship's Anchor

After Ernie and I visited with Mrs. Claibourne and Mrs. Holloman, we headed back to the Ship's Anchor for more tea. We drove slowly along the narrow, hilly island roads. The tall pine trees made a dark ceiling on both sides of the road. I could see ferns and pale flowers in the dim woods. "What hard work it must have been for the pioneers to clear this land!" I said to Ernie.

While we waited for our tea at the Ship's Anchor, Ernie and I wrote down the names of our parents and our aunts, uncles, grandparents and a few great-grandparents. We told stories about each of these people.

"I know a lot more about Sylvia Stark than I do about my great-grandmother," I told Ernie. "My great-grandmother came over from Ireland and married an Irish minister. They were poor and had a lot of kids who liked to make trouble."

"My great-grandparents lived in Mississippi and then their kids moved to Chicago," Ernie said. "There was an Irish man and a Cherokee woman in my family somewhere. I think my mother has a family tree that goes back five generations to slaves and slave owners."

The longer Ernie and I talked, the more stories we remembered. They were stories about men and women in our families, people who were not famous but who made choices and changed the world around them in small ways. They were people who made history by living their lives.